what do
i do
when...

answering your **TOUGHEST**
questions about
Friends

by kevin moore

D1318640

Harrison House
Tulsa, Oklahoma

15 14 13 12 11   10 9 8 7 6 5 4 3 2

What Do I Do When?
Answering Your Toughest Questions About Friends
ISBN 13: 978-1-57794-962-6
ISBN 10: 1-57794-962-5
Copyright © 2009 by Kevin Moore
P.O. Box 692032
Tulsa, Oklahoma 74169-2032

Published by Harrison House Publishers
P.O. Box 35035
Tulsa, Oklahoma 74135
www.harrisonhouse.com

Table of Contents

Introduction

No matter what race, social status, or religious background you come from, you have three things in common with every other person on planet Earth.

First of all, you have questions. Like everybody else, you have times in your life when you don't understand what's going on, why something happened, or what to do in a certain situation. From time to time, you have questions.

Second, you want a friend. Friends can be, without a doubt, the most influential part of your life. Think about it. Your friends affect the clothes you wear, the games you play, the music you listen to, and the things you choose to believe. *Friend* is one of the most powerful words in the English language.

Third, like everyone else on this rotating rock known as Earth, you have questions about your friends. You love your friends; you care about your friends. Because of this, at times your friends make your world incredibly fun, and at other times they drive you stinking crazy. Especially when you have absolutely no clue why they did what they did or how you should respond to what they've done.

That's why I wrote this book. I want to help you find answers to some of the questions you might have about your friends. I want to assist you in dealing with some of the issues that come up from time to time between you and the most influential people in your life. Now, I'll probably not hit all of your questions, but for the ones I do, I sure hope this helps.

May *His* best be yours,
—*Kevin Moore*

What Do I
Do When...

My Friends
Don't Want
Jesus?

I want to start this book off by letting you know I am a Christian. And by that, I mean according to Romans 10:9, I have confessed with my mouth that Jesus Christ is Lord and I believe in my heart that God raised Jesus from the dead. I am a Christian.

Now, I don't know for sure, but most likely if you're reading this chapter, you're a Christian, too. You may not be perfect. In fact, I'm positive you aren't. However, you probably believe in God and love Jesus.

Most likely, even though you're a Christian and love Jesus, you probably have friends or family members who, for whatever reason, aren't Christians and don't want to be. Either they don't know much about God, or they do and for some reason just don't seem interested in becoming followers of Christ.

I'm sure you know someone who doesn't want Jesus. Have you ever stopped to think of why? Why wouldn't someone want Him? He *is* the Son of God, for crying out loud. Jesus loved us enough to become one of us. He lived a perfect life. He healed a ton of people while He was here. He willingly took the penalty for our sin, which was a gruesome death on the cross. He was put in the grave for three days, and then He kicked the devil's when God raised Him up from the dead.

I mean, how could someone not be crazy about this guy? How in the world would anyone not want Jesus? It's something that you and I, people who are followers of Christ, sometimes have a hard time understanding, but let's try to put ourselves in their shoes for a minute.

Let's say I take you to a room that's pitch-black. I mean, this room is so dark you can't even see the hand in front of your face. So I take you by the hand and lead you into this totally dark room. Once inside, I tell you there's someone in this room who is absolutely perfect for you.

If you're a guy, there's a girl in this pitch-black room who's flat-out, steaming hot. She has beautiful hair, a great smile, a fabulous body, and an unbelievable personality. She is perfect. I tell you, "Now, you can't see her, but trust me—she is *good.*"

If you're a girl, the guy in this room is six foot two and a chiseled one hundred eighty-five pounds of pure *hunk.* He is great-looking, smart, fun, and very wealthy. I tell you, "You cannot see him, but trust me—he is a real hottie."

Now, here's the deal. The next thing I say is this: "The person in this dark room is ready right now to say, 'I do,' and marry you. You cannot and have not ever seen this person, but trust me—you will love this person."

Let me ask you a question: Would you do it? Would you marry this person, sight unseen? Would you make a permanent, life-long commitment to someone you've never even met before?

No! There's no way! Right? You've never even seen the girl; you've never even seen the guy. How in the world can you make a commitment to somebody you don't even know?

It's the exact same way with your friends who don't want Jesus. You see, the reason they don't want Him, the reason they're not willing to make a lifelong commitment to Him is not because He's not good, gracious, powerful, and kind. Jesus is all of those things and more. The reason they're uninterested in committing to Him is that they haven't seen Him for themselves.

Your friends and family members who don't know Jesus are most likely great people. However, they live in a world that's spiritually pitch-black. The only way they'll ever really want Jesus is if they can somehow see Him. If they could see Jesus, they would love Him, they would want Him, and they would follow Him, just as you and I have already decided to do.

So how do they see Him?

Well, what do you do when you're in a dark room and you want to see? You turn on a light.

Listen to what Jesus says in Matthew 5:14-16:

> "You are the light of the world. A city on a hill cannot be hidden. Neither do people light a lamp and put it under a bowl. Instead they put it on its stand, and it gives light to everyone in the house. In the same way,

let your light shine before men, that they may see
your good deeds and praise your Father in heaven."

In this passage, Jesus is saying that *you* are the light in the
room of your friends' lives. You are the light that is supposed
to shine so your friends can actually see Jesus.

So what do you do when your friends don't want Jesus?

Turn on the light in your life. Here are five ways to shine
your L.I.G.H.T.

Love

The first way you can shine your light for your friends to see
Jesus is by learning to love them. Love is a very vague word,
isn't it? I mean, what is love? Is love a feeling? Is love all
about sex? Is love all about family? Can you fall in love? And
if you can, is it possible to fall out of love? Is love an action?
And if so, what actions actually show true love? What in the
world is love?

Well, I think love can be summed up in a short sentence that
Jesus once said: "Do to others as you would have them do to
you" (Luke 6:31). The Golden Rule, as this is commonly
known, sums up the very essence of love.

In order to show your friends Jesus, all you need to do is start
treating them the way you want to be treated. If you want
your friends to be patient with you, be patient with them. If

you want your friends to forgive you, forgive them. If you don't want them to lie to you, then don't lie to them. If you don't like to be yelled at, then don't yell at your friends. If you want your friends to be real and authentic Christians someday, then you need to make sure your private life lines up with your public persona.

Caring enough about other people to treat them the way you want to be treated is the very essence of love—and love is an extremely rare commodity these days. Showing real, authentic love to your friends by simply treating them the way you want to be treated yourself will begin to open their eyes to who the Father really is—a good God who loves and cares about them, just like you do.

Invest

. . . .

The second way you can shine your light for your friends to see Jesus is by learning to invest in them. When you read through the pages of Scripture, you will see that Jesus was a big-time investor. No, stocks and bonds were not His deal; people were His investment of choice.

Jesus was constantly giving. He gave His time. He gave His energy. There were times when He gave food to the hungry, and other times He gave sight to the blind. Today He is still giving. He gives hope, love, joy, peace, self-control, and for-giveness to anyone who asks. Jesus is a big-time giver.

As a Christian, a Christ follower, you are supposed to emulate—or be just like—Jesus. So if He invested in the people around Him, it only makes sense that you should give to those who are closest to you.

What can you give? How about a smile? A hello? A conversation? Maybe some good advice or forgiveness when it's needed? Life is about much more than you, so find a friend and give.

Go to God

The third way you can shine your light for your friends to see Jesus is by going to God. It will take a huge change of heart for your friends to go from not caring at all about God to actually wanting to give their entire lives to Him. It'll be such a big thing, in fact, that there's no way you can make it happen. Only God can change someone's heart. So go to Him in prayer, and begin to ask Him for three things.

1. To Help You Live Right

First, ask God to help you live right. Remember: Jesus said that you are the light of the world and when people see your good works they will glorify your Father in heaven.

With all the junk you live with every single day, living right and doing good deeds aren't as easy as they seem. You probably need a little help. So start praying that God will help you live the way you need to live so He can change your friends' hearts in the process.

2. To Soften Their Hearts

Second, ask Him to soften their hearts. My wife is a gardener. Every year, she plants a little garden in our back yard. Before she plants the seeds in the ground, she has me get out my tiller and begin to till up the soil. As the ground is being chopped up, the soil gets softer and softer. Once the ground is ready, Veronica goes out and plants the seed, waters the garden, and watches it grow.

It's the same with your friends. If they're ever going to accept Jesus, they need to have soft hearts. Now, you don't want to get the tiller out and run over your friends with it. That would be pretty sick—fun possibly, but definitely sick.

Remember: You cannot change or alter your friends' hearts. But you can begin to ask God to soften them so when you live a good life in front of them or tell them about Jesus, the things they hear and see will have an eternal impact on them.

3. To Open Their Eyes

Third, ask God to open your friends' eyes. Remember: your friends are living in a totally dark spiritual room. It's very hard for them to see Jesus. It's easy for them to see church, religion, or people who say they're Christians but don't live like it. But it's very hard for them to see Jesus.

Because of this, not only should you live the way Jesus would live; you should pray that God would supernaturally open your friends' spiritual eyes so they can see Jesus in you.

Help Point Them to Jesus

You've seen how to love, invest in, and go to God for your friends. The fourth way you can shine your light for your friends is by helping to point them to Jesus. As you do this, remember: Your actions speak louder than your words.

Let's say your coach just came up to you and said you were not only the best player on the team—you were the best player *he had ever seen.* I know it sounds crazy, but track along with me just a minute. The dude comes up and says you are flat-out the absolute best player. In fact, he says no one else has ever even come close to your skill level.

However, when the game starts, you find yourself riding the pine on the bench. Then, to make matters worse, halfway through the game, your coach looks down at you and says with a huge smile, "You're the best player I've ever seen. The best!" Then he looks away and doesn't put you in the game.

Would you believe what he's just said to you? Would you really think he truly believed you were the best player he'd ever seen?

No?

Why?

Because your butt's falling asleep while you sit on the bench. Right? He hasn't even put you in the game! How can you be the best player if you're rotting on the sidelines? Your coach's actions speak louder than words.

This is exactly how it works with someone who doesn't know Christ. Your actions will always speak louder than your words to this person. If you say you're a Christ follower, but you cheat on a test, your actions have spoken louder than your words. If you say you're a Christian, but you consistently lie to get yourself out of trouble, your actions have spoken louder than your words. If you tell everyone you love God, but you're always dogging on the kid no one likes, once again your actions have spoken louder than your words.

Your friend is observing more how you live than what you say. So if you have a friend who doesn't know Christ, just remember: Your actions always speak louder than your words. Help point your friend to Jesus more by what you do than by what you say.

You know, it's really not that hard to point someone to Jesus in your actions. In fact, it could be as easy as going up to the kid no one else in school likes and simply saying, "Hello." Or by owning up to a mistake instead of lying or trying to push your mistake off on someone else. Or by shutting your mouth when you have the juiciest piece of gossip the school has ever seen since little Timmy Smith pooped his pants in science class.

Why? Why be nice to the "loser" kid? Why own up to your mistakes? Why not pass along some sweet info?

It's because your friends need Jesus, and God has placed you in their lives to point them to Him. If you really want your friends to know how good, gracious, and kind Jesus really is, follow these words attributed to Saint Francis of Assisi:

> Preach the Gospel at all times. When necessary, use words.

Take Them to Church

The fifth way you can shine your light for your friends to see Jesus is by taking them to church.

There are some things we were not meant to do alone; certain things we just don't want to do by ourselves. Take movies, for example. Have you ever been to the movies by yourself? Most people don't like going to movies alone. I'm not really sure why, but movies just seem to be more enjoyable when you have someone with you.

Video games are the same way. *Rock Band, Guitar Hero, Madden,* and *Halo* – you can play any of these games alone, but they're a lot more fun when a buddy is over or you're kickin' some random kid's tailbone online. Right?

Sometimes I think girls weren't meant to go to the bathroom alone. This is something I've never understood. A girl will look at one of her friends and say, "Hey, Sheila, I gotta go to the bathroom. You wanna come with me?" I've always wondered what happens in there. Is there music playing, couches you sit on, some free buffet bar, or what? You'll never see that from a guy: "Hey, Steve. Dude, I've got to go hit the john. Why don't you come to the stall next to mine, and let's talk about football." It'll never happen. Never. But with girls, it happens all the time. Girls, for whatever reason, apparently were not designed to go to the bathroom alone.

We were not designed to do everything by ourselves. Some things are more fun on a team, some things are better with a friend, and other things are just way too big for us to do all alone.

Here's a great example of that. A few years ago, I was coming home from a speaking trip. After I landed at the airport, my wife, Veronica, called and asked me to run to my favorite store on planet Earth (Wal-Mart™) to pick up a few things we needed. On my way home from the store, my car started running really crazy, smoking, and all kinds of junk. I pulled the car over, let it cool down, and then kept driving home.

After walking into the house, I commented to my wife, "The car's running a little funny. I'll get it checked out this week." About thirty minutes later, I just happened to look out my window and, to my horror, my car was on fire! Five-foot flames were shooting out of the hood. My beautiful 1997 purple Plymouth Breeze was a blazing inferno!

I ran down the stairs and told Veronica, "The car's on fire!"

She said, "What?"

I said, "The car's on fire!"

My oldest son, Jordan, got up and ran out to get the water hose. My other son, Logan, ran out the door and across the yard to the neighbor's house, screaming, "We're gonna die! Somebody's gonna die!"

My five-year-old daughter, Mikayla, who's been raised to call on Jesus in times of trouble, ran out to the garage in her pajamas and started pacing around in circles with her hands up in the air, shouting, "Jesus! Oh, Jesus! Help us, Jesus!"

It was a mess. The fire was growing larger and larger; the flames were billowing out the sides. *Bam! Bam!* The tires exploded one by one. It was getting totally out of control. And there I stood about three feet from the flames, holding nothing but a small garden hose and trying to put out this giant explosion of flames in my front yard.

Needless to say, it wasn't going well. Things were getting scary. I needed some backup, so we called the fire department. When the fire trucks and firefighters showed up, they had the fire under control and out in just a few minutes.

You know what? It's the same way in your walk with Christ. Right after Jesus rose from the dead, He gave His disciples—including us—an assignment. This assignment shows His heart and His passion for people. You may or may not have heard of it before. It's called the Great Commission, and in it, He said, "Go into all the world and preach the good news to all creation" (Mark 16:15). With this statement, Jesus was letting us know that all creation—the world around us, the people we see every day, including our friends—need to hear the good news about Christ.

Let's be honest. That's a *huge* responsibility. Reaching a friend? Changing an eternal destiny? That's a huge deal. We weren't meant to do that alone. Like my car catching on fire, the Great Commission is too big for you or for me to handle alone. It's too big for anyone to handle alone.

That's one of the reasons God created this entity called *the Church*. Without a doubt, He wants us to reach out to those closest to us, but He doesn't expect or even want us to do it all alone.

We see this from the very outset of the Christian faith—back when this Christian thing was just getting started. A lot of people had come to faith. However, just like you and me, the people who were following Christ were surrounded by individuals who still didn't know Him or really even want Him. So this is what the followers of Christ did:

> Every day they continued to meet together in the temple courts. They broke bread in their homes and ate together with glad and sincere hearts, praising God and enjoying the favor of all the people. And the Lord added to their number daily those who were being saved.

> Acts 2:46-47

Here's what was going on. The people who personally knew Jesus would go to church. While they were there, they would sing, they would pray, and they would learn more about God. But afterward, they would be meeting in houses all across the city. While there, they'd invite their saved and unsaved friends to join them for dinner. They ate, had fun, told stories, talked about life, and talked about God. Then they'd invite their unsaved friends to join them in church the next time they were going.

While at church, the unsaved heard about the love of God, were exposed to His goodness, and because they saw Jesus in the friendliness of their friends and the teaching of Scripture at church, they accepted Him as the Lord of their lives. Because individuals and the church purposely worked together, lives were saved and the Great Commission was fulfilled.

This thing of turning on the light and showing your friends Jesus' goodness is way too big for you to do alone. But on the flip side, it is way too personal to be done just by the church. By doing your part and allowing the church to do its part, you will be sharing your faith the way God intended it to be done: together.

How to Lead a Friend to Christ

Let's say you're a Christian and you shined your light to a good buddy who doesn't know Jesus. Now, because of the way you've lived, your friend actually wants to be a Christian, too. What do you do now?

One of the best ways to bring your friends to Jesus is by taking them down the Roman Road. Now, the Roman Road is not some road in Italy that Roman soldiers used to walk down. No, it's actually three verses in the Bible that will lead your friend to a personal relationship with Jesus.

If you have a friend who wants to accept Jesus as Savior, go to a quiet place where you and your friend can talk, and then follow these three steps.

1. Let Them Know Everybody Sins

Romans 3:23 says, "For all have sinned and fall short of the glory of God." The first way to lead a friend to Christ is to let him or her know that everyone, including you, has made some big-time mistakes and fallen a little short of the standard God has for people to live. We have all sinned.

2. Let Them Know God Loved Us Enough To Die for Us

The second thing you can do to lead your friend to Christ is to explain how much God loves us. Romans 5:8 says, "God demonstrates his own love for us in this: While we were still sinners, Christ died for us."

As you talk to your friends about becoming followers of Christ, explain that God knew they were going to sin and mess up, but He loves them anyway. Because sin has to be punished, God sent His Son, Jesus, to take their punishment for sin by dying for them on a cross.

3. Pray Together

Let's say you've spoken with your friend about these things and your friend wants to follow Christ. The third step you can take is to pray together. Romans 10:9-10 says, "If you confess with your mouth, 'Jesus is Lord,' and believe in your heart that God raised him from the dead, you will be saved. For it is with your heart that you believe and are justified, and it is with your mouth that you confess and are saved."

This is a huge deal. This Scripture lets us know exactly how to be saved. First of all, we confess with our mouths that Jesus Christ is more than a good person who lived a long time ago; He is actually Lord. Secondly, if we believe in our hearts that He not only died for our sins but was also raised up from the dead, we'll be saved.

Let your friends know that in spite of all the mistakes they've made in the past, God wants to forgive them. By accepting what Jesus did for them on the cross, they can have a brand new life in Christ.

Here's a prayer you can lead your friend in:

Dear heavenly Father, today I confess that I am a sinner. I ask You to forgive me for all the mistakes I have ever made. I accept the price Christ paid for my sins on the cross, and I believe without any doubts that He has been raised up from the dead. From this day on, I will live a life that gives You glory. I am saved—not because of what I do, but because of what Jesus Christ has done for me. Thank You, Lord, for saving me, in Jesus' name. Amen.

It's just that simple. I pray that you will let your light shine to your friends—love, invest, go to God in prayer, help point them to Jesus, and then take them to church. I pray you'll have tons of opportunities to lead the people closest to you into a personal relationship with Jesus Christ.

What Do I
Do When...

My Friend
Is Mean?

Sometimes friends are mean. It's painful when they are, and their meanness can come out in different ways. Do you have someone close to you who fits any of the following descriptions?

1. Selfish

Do you know people who live like everything is all about them—their fun, their plans, their music, their clothes, their stuff, and on and on—all about them?

2. Lying

Do you have friends who are in the habit of lying? You never know for sure if they're telling you the truth because nine times out of ten they aren't. They stretch the truth, they bend the truth. But for some reason, they never seem to tell the truth.

3. Manipulating

Do you know any manipulators? These people are real masterminds. They always seem to be one step ahead of the game. No matter what the situation, they always end up getting exactly what they want. The problem is that they leave a pretty big wake of pain and stress wherever they go.

4. Two-Faced

Do you have any friends who are two-faced? Around you, they're one way; but around someone else, they're something totally different. These people are real chameleons. They blend in seamlessly with whatever crowd they're in.

5. Screaming

Do you know any screamers? Like a volcano, these friends could explode at any time. You have to walk softly around them at all times. They're totally fine one moment; then the next thing you know, they're spewing their hot lava of hatred all over you.

What To Do When Your Friend Is Mean

Now, I'm sure the people you know who have some of these characteristics have some other qualities that are pretty cool. For example, maybe they're really funny or maybe they have some sweet hair. Let's be totally honest here, though, if you have a lying, selfish, manipulating, two-faced friend who's always screaming at you, you've got a pretty mean friend.

So what do you do when your friend is mean? Well, here are a few ideas.

1. Ignore

Your first option when a friend is mean is to ignore it. It's hard, but it's a good way to calm things down really quickly.

A few years ago, my sons and I were cutting the back acre and a half of our property. We had not mowed it in several months, and the grass was extremely tall. After getting it all mowed, we raked it all up into one huge, monstrous mound of grass.

We lived way out in the country, so I thought the best thing to do would be to set fire to it and burn the whole thing down. So I got some matches and threw them in at the bottom of the pile. Well, some of the grass was still a little green, so the fire didn't really take off all that well. There was just some smoke coming out from the bottom of the mound.

I got this great idea to pour gasoline on the mound to make it actually catch fire. I went and grabbed a five-gallon can of gasoline and began to pour it on the mound. I started at the top and began to work my way down to the bottom. Everything was going fine until I hit the area where smoke was coming out. Then *BOOOOOM!* The entire six-foot mound of grass exploded into a towering inferno of flames!

I jumped back and started to run away, then I realized flames were shooting out of the nozzle of the gas can in my hand. Like the brave and intelligent man that I am, I started to scream and then took off running, still holding onto the burning gas can. This made the flames shoot out even farther, so I stopped running, threw the can down onto the lawn, and watched the fire go out.

Here's a little lesson you can learn from my stupidity. When you have friends who are always manipulating, yelling, complaining, or looking for some juicy info to spread around, your friends are like the mound of grass in my lawn. They have a small fire burning way down deep inside of them that they need to deal with. When you play into their complaining, yelling, or gossiping, you're throwing gasoline on their fire and *BOOOOOM!* You've just made their "mean" issue bigger, stronger, and more dangerous than it was before.

Proverbs 12:16 says, "A fool shows his annoyance at once, but a prudent man overlooks an insult." What God is basically saying is that if you have a friend who's kind of mean, you should ignore it. Don't play up to it; try your best to overlook it. Making an issue of some mean thing someone is doing is like throwing gas on a fire.

Your "mean" friends are looking for an outlet. They're looking for someone who will listen to them complain, for someone who will listen to their juicy piece of gossip, for someone who will get up in their face and want to fight.

When your friends do this, don't give in to them. Ignore them. Eventually the fire will die down. Then you'll go on your way, with or without them, and the problem will be gone.

2. Confront

Ecclesiastes 3:1 says, "There is a time for everything, and a season for every activity under heaven." God teaches us in His Word that there is a time and a place for everything. There is a time to ignore the "mean" issue that your friend is struggling with, and there is a time to take the second option of confronting the issue.

Have you ever been out to eat with someone and he had some food on his face? Dude, that is so sick. Isn't it? He has absolutely no idea it's there. He's talking, laughing, and stuffing his face. All the while, he's rocking some mustard and ketchup, with chunks of burger mixed in, right on the side of his mouth.

In that situation, what's the right thing to do? Sit there and let him keep looking stupid? Sit there and keep being grossed out by what you're looking at? No, the right thing to do is to be honest with him and let him know he has something gross stuck to his face.

It's the same thing with your friends who are constantly unleashing the monster of "mean" on you. Maybe you've tried to ignore and overlook it, but it's still there. Maybe it's starting to affect you and your friendship. If you're in this situation, you, as a friend, have the responsibility to sit down and have an honest conversation with them.

Now, it should be a conversation, not a yelling match or a huge fight. As a friend, let them know what they're doing and how it's affecting you. Then together, start to deal with the problem. This is how you try to put out the fire.

3. Leave

So you have friends who are pretty mean. You've hung out together for years, and you don't know what your life would be like without them. However, the way they act is flat-out killing you. You feel like they're always manipulating you so they can get their way. You do one thing they don't like, and they just go off on this tirade of anger and yelling.

What can you do? You've tried to ignore it, but that didn't work. You've sat down with them and had a good pow-wow, letting them know what they are doing and how it affects you, but the "mean" keeps on coming.

Now it's really starting to get to you. Things aren't the same as they used to be. Your stress level is through the roof, and you don't know what to do.

Well, listen to these words found in Proverbs 22:10: "Drive out the mocker, and out goes strife; quarrels and insults are ended."

There you have it. There's your answer. If you've tried everything, and your friends are still as mean as Marilyn Manson (I don't know if this old-school rocker is actually mean, but he looks like it), then you have to get them out of your life. Stop hanging out with them, period. End of discussion. When you stop spending time with the people who are being mean, your life is going to go a lot smoother.

So what do you do when your friends are mean? Try your best to *ignore* it. Let it die down on its own. If that doesn't work, *confront* them. Let them know exactly what they're doing and how it's affecting you. And if that doesn't work, you need to *leave* the friendship. Stop hanging out with them; stop exchanging phone calls and text messages. I know that's a hard thing to do, but the truth is that life has enough stress without having to put up with your friends' messes—so move on.

What Do I
Do When...

I've Been
Stabbed in
the Back?

I'm the type of person who doesn't let people get close to me all that easily. Don't get me wrong, I'm not some hermit who lives up in the mountains and only comes down to get the bare essentials of life—like Mountain Dew® and pork rinds. No, I have a lot of friends; however, I only have a few friends in my inner circle. Because of this, the people who are close to me play important roles in my life.

A few years ago, I had a friend I let into my inner circle; in fact, we were extremely close. Every weekend, our families were together. We went to movies and went out to eat together. We were so close, in fact, that we even did the whole holiday scene together: turkey, exchanging gifts, the whole deal. We were very good friends.

I guess that's why it hurt so badly. I won't go into details, but let me just say that my friend said some things that were extremely painful and untrue about me to pretty much every-one I knew. I'll never forget it.... The pain of the knife going right in my back was excruciating.

Has that ever happened to you? Have you ever been stabbed in the back? I'm sure you have, and I'm sure it hurt when it all went down. Right? Well, what do you do when that happens? What do you do when someone close to you stabs you in the back?

Get Your Facts Straight

The first thing you need to do if you think your friend has stabbed you in the back is to make sure you get your facts straight. Deuteronomy 19:15 says, "One witness is not enough to convict a man accused of any crime or offense he may have committed. A matter must be established by the testimony of two or three witnesses." This passage is saying that before you accuse, confront, or just start going off on your friend because you heard he or she stabbed you in the back, you need to get all your facts straight.

It's not a good idea to take as fact something one person says about your friend. It very well may be true, or the person might have gotten it totally wrong. So find out. Talk to some other people who were around and see if what you heard is really true. However, if you yourself did not see or hear what your friend did, the best way to find out what went down is just to go up to your friend and ask.

Just be sure to get your facts straight.

Don't Overreact

If you've checked your facts and discovered your friend really has done you wrong, the second thing you should do is to avoid overreacting. One of the biggest mistakes people make when something goes wrong is to overreact. Here are a few things you don't want to do when you've been stabbed in the back.

1. Don't Go Postal

When the knife gets plunged deep in your back, don't go all postal on your friend and the people around you. Don't start sobbing, crying, throwing stuff across the room, screaming, and yelling. That doesn't really help the situation. I mean, come on, how is busting a big hole in the wall of your bedroom going to help what went down between you and your friend? It won't, but now not only will you have some friend issues, you'll have your mom and dad all ticked off as well.

I know you're hurt and probably angry, but relax. Going postal only makes things worse.

2. Don't Say Things You Don't Mean

A lot of times when we get hurt, we say some stuff we don't really mean. And after the issue dies down, which it will, we're filled with regret for saying some pretty stupid stuff ourselves. So take this word to the wise: If you don't mean it, don't say it.

3. Don't Repay Wrong With Wrong

If you hurt me, I'll hurt you. That's typically what we think and how we live. And to be honest, it's pretty stupid, because when that's your life's motto, in the end you are actually only hurting yourself.

Jesus once said, "Give and it will be given to you" (Luke 6:38). Whatever you do to your friends, your friends will do to you. So if they hurt you and then you hurt them back, what do you think they're going to do to you? Hurt you again. Because they hurt you again, you hurt them again. And what do you think they're going to do to you? Hurt you again. Because they hurt you, you hurt them... and the cycle continues.

This is dumb. When your friend hurts you, don't overreact and repay one wrong with another, because all you're doing is hurting yourself all over again. Stop the cycle, and don't overreact.

How To Keep From Overreacting

So how do you keep from overreacting when you think your friend has stabbed you in the back? I know it's not easy, but here are some ideas to help you keep your cool.

1. Think

The first way to keep from overreacting is to stop and think. Before you run off and react to something you've just heard, take a minute or two to think it through. Here are three great questions to ask yourself when you're thinking it through.

- Does this really sound like something your friend would do?

- Have you given your friend any reasons to do this?

- Based on everything you know, what is the best way to respond?

If you ask yourself these three questions, it will give you time to think and avoid overreacting. Take some time to stop and think.

2. Pray

After stopping to think, the second way to keep from overreacting is to pray. I know this whole big thing just went down, but you don't have to figure it out all on our own. To keep yourself from overreacting, you can look outside yourself for help. You see, all throughout history when big things went down, people turned to God, and He always helped them. If He helped them, I'm pretty sure He could help you, too.

It's hard to not overreact when you feel you're facing a huge problem alone, but remember: You're not alone. So take a few minutes and talk to God about the issue, and ask Him for some help.

3. Respond

After thinking and praying, the third way to avoid overreacting is to respond. Your response will depend on how
big the knife they used to stab you with is. Your response
may have to be face to face, it could be a quick text to
see what's up, or you may have to get some adults in on
the situation.

Every situation is a little different, but remember, never
respond until you have taken some time to think and pray.

Forgive

After you've gotten your facts straight and kept yourself from
overreacting, the next thing you need to do to keep your cool
when you've been backstabbed is to forgive. This can be a
pretty tough thing to do. I know from experience. When my
friend stabbed me pretty good, I was shocked, angry, and
upset—but mostly I was hurt. How could he do this to me?
We were friends. But then I started to think of all the wrong
things I have done in my life and how every time I've asked
Jesus to forgive me, He always has. I remember thinking, *If
Jesus will forgive me for all the junk I've done, surely I can
forgive my friend for this one thing.*

So that night I thought about the situation, I prayed and asked
God for wisdom, and the next day I responded with forgiveness. I remember sitting down and calmly talking with my

friend. I confronted him with what he did, why it was wrong, and how it made me feel. He apologized, said he was sorry, and asked me to forgive him.

And you know what? I did.

Right then and there, I chose to forgive my friend, just like Christ had forgiven me. Because I did, that allowed me to move on with my life.

Move On

After you've gotten your facts straight, kept yourself from over-reacting, and done the hard work of forgiving, it's time to move on. Life is pretty short. At best, you're only going to live about eighty years here on this spinning rock. Right? So why waste precious time holding onto the past, bringing up hurtful memories, and being ticked off for something you can't really do anything about?

If you have friends who have stabbed you in the back, get all your facts straight, don't overreact, forgive when they ask, and then move on.

You've got a great life ahead of you. Take these steps to get over the pain of past stabs in the back, and then keep moving forward.

What Do I Do When...

I Don't Fit In?

It was a moment that I will never forget. We had just moved into town, and I was the new guy. I and several other people had gotten together for an impromptu meeting. At the end of the meeting, we all stood up and started walking out the door.

As we were all walking out, one guy with his back to me looked at a few of his friends and said, "Hey, I'm hungry. You guys want to go get some lunch?"

They all replied, "Sure. Where do you want to go? Ah, man, there's this sweet place a few blocks from here that you'll love."

As we all kept walking, the four people standing beside me were talking, laughing, and making plans to grab some grub together. Even though I was walking alongside them, no one ever asked me if I wanted to join them. No one acknowledged my presence or even looked my way. It was as if I wasn't even there.

As I stood there watching the four friends get into the car and drive off together, three words came to my mind: *Dude, this stinks!*

Has that ever happened to you? Have you ever been in a situation where you just didn't fit in? Everyone is tight. Everyone is close. Everyone knows all the inside jokes. Everyone...except you.

You're on the outside looking in. You're there, but no one even notices you. That is a horrible feeling, isn't it?

We all want to be accepted. We all want to be liked. We all want to be the center of attention, the life of the party. But it's not always going to be that way. In fact, it's not supposed to be that way.

If your goal in life is to always fit in and always be accepted no matter whom you are around, you're going to be a very miserable person. Because if you do that, you'll never actually be who you are. You'll only be what you think other people want you to be. After a while, that will get pretty old.

So what do you do when you're in a situation where you just don't fit in? Well, here are some things to keep in mind.

Don't Try So Hard

You know that kid at school who wears way too much cologne? The kid you can smell when he is a good thirty feet away? The kid who has a huge bottle of Drakkar in his gym locker and a giant tub of Sex Panther in his hall locker? The kid you can probably smell right now?

Yeah, that kid.

Why does he wear so much cologne? He wears it because he thinks it will draw the chicks to him like flies. Right? Does it work? Does slapping on two handfuls of cheap cologne actually attract beautiful ladies, or does it repel them?

I'll tell you. It repels them. Why does everyone turn and run from him rather than toward him? Because he is trying way too hard. Let's face it. The dude stinks!

It is the same with fitting in with the people around you. The more you try—the more you exaggerate who you are or try to be what you think they want you to be—the more they will run from you rather than toward you. The harder you try, the more you'll push people away.

Six Friendship Repellents

When people try too hard, they generally start to turn into people who repel friends rather than attract them. I'll give you six examples of people who repel friendship.

1. Ms. Manipulator

First on the list of friendship repellents is Ms. Manipulator. On the outside, this person is very friendly, very complimentary, and seems to be a real team player. But on the inside, she has her own agenda. Always shifting, always working on angles, always playing one person against the other—she's always working to get what she wants.

Ms. Manipulator plays the game by her rules, but in the end she's the one getting played, because she will be all alone.

2. Captain Complainer

Second on the list of friendship repellents is Captain Complainer. This guy is constantly complaining. He always says things like this: "I don't have enough money." "My clothes are not as nice as yours." "I wish I lived in your neighborhood; mine stinks." "My girlfriend is so ugly, but she was the only one who would go out with me."

Here's the deal about this guy. First, nobody wants to be around a Billy Bummer. No one wants to be around someone who's always complaining, always down, always bummed about something. People want to have fun, and this guy is not fun.

Second, people get turned off by Captain Complainer because, after a while, they catch on to his game. They start to realize he is always saying how bad things are for him so that others will have to tell him that he is wrong, that things are really good for him. He has a lot of money, his clothes are really nice, his neighborhood is pretty sweet, and his girlfriend is extremely hot. People want to hang out with other people who are confident in who they are. Because this guy has to keep being propped up, eventually people just get tired and leave Captain Complainer to sail the seas of life all alone.

3. Ms. Do-You-Know-How-Much-This-Cost?

The next friendship repellent is the person who cannot go through a conversation without dropping how much she spent on something or other. She's Ms. Do-You-Know-How-Much-This-Cost? You know the type. You walk into her living room and comment on how nice her TV is and she says, "Thanks. We got a great deal on it. It was only five thousand dollars." Or she walks up to you at school and you make a passing comment about her shoes, and she takes ten minutes to point out when and where she bought them and exactly how much they cost.

The thing that Ms. Do-You-Know-How-Much-This-Cost? fails to realize is that *no one cares!* No one cares that her sunglasses were $50. No one cares that her shirt was a steal at $25 or their registered pooch cost $500. Nobody cares, except for her.

She mistakenly thinks that everyone loves money and that if she lets people know how much money she has, then they will want to hang out with her. But after a while, Ms. Do-You-Know-How-Much-This-Cost? starts to smell like Sex Panther and begins to repel the very people she wants to get close to.

4. Mr. Mean

The fourth friendship repellent is Mr. Mean. Because this one's so good at putting down others, pointing out flaws, and using other people's huge mistakes as ways to get laughs, Mr. Mean is usually a very funny person with a lot of friends, at least for a while.

But after continually being the target of all his jokes, one by one people start to walk away from Mr. Mean and begin to hang out with someone who is actually funny and not just cruel.

5. Ms. Gossip

Fifth up on the list of friendship repellents is Ms. Gossip. You've met this one, and her behavior doesn't welcome true friendship. Think of it this way.

Let's say your grandma just sent you a check for $50 totally out of the blue. Grandmas are good like that, aren't they? You're amped up and can't wait to spend the cash, so you drop a text to your best friend telling her to meet you at the mall in thirty minutes. When you get to the mall, you show your friend the money and start walking to your favorite store. As you're walking, your friend asks to see your cash again, you pull it out of your pocket, and as you show her your money, to your shock your friend grabs the cash and runs off with it.

That's the type of person who is not going to have many friends. Right? Well, Ms. Gossip is that friend. She's the type of person who takes something that does not belong to her and runs off with it, sharing it with everyone she knows.

People don't like thieves, and that is exactly what Ms. Gossip is.

6. Mr. Super Spiritual

The sixth friendship repellent is Mr. Super Spiritual. Have you ever known someone who was better than you at everything, and they let you know it? Did you like him? I didn't think so.

Mr. Super Spiritual is extremely close to God, and he's not afraid to let you know it. While he's been reading the Bible, memorizing Scriptures and going on mission's trips, though, he has somehow forgotten all about a pretty important phrase in the Bible: "Do to others as you would have them do to you" (Luke 6:31). Because of his holier-than-thou attitude, it won't take long before not even God wants to be close to this guy.

Are You a Friendship Repellent?

If, for whatever reason, you look at these six people and you see a little bit of yourself in one of them, that very well could be the reason you have not been fitting in lately. If you have been one of these friendship repellents, right now ask God to forgive you and to help you become a real friend.

One thing you'll learn in life is that you've got to be a friend to get a friend. Proverbs 18:24 says that a man who has friends must first show himself friendly.

Think of five words to define the word "friendly." Go ahead. Stop reading for a minute, and think of five words.

Okay. You got them? Good.

Let me ask you a question. Were any of the words you chose "mean," "gossip," "liar," "cheater," "manipulator," or "hypocrite"?

No, I didn't think so. If they were, you may want to get your head checked, because you could be a bit warped in the melon.

You see, the Bible says that if you want to have friends, you must first be friendly. You have to have some qualities inside of you that people are looking for in a friend.

Five Qualities That Attract Friends

A few years ago, my wife picked up something known as "the world's strongest magnet." In a tiny little box were these two magnets. When she brought it home and I saw how small the magnets were, I was sure she had totally wasted her money. There was no way these magnets were the strongest in the world.

Then I tried to pull the two magnets apart. I remember grabbing both magnets and pulling and pulling as hard as I possibly could. Dude, that magnet was strong! There was no way they were coming apart. I could not separate them.

Did you know there are certain qualities that you can begin to cultivate in your life that will act like a magnet, attracting people to you? These qualities, although small, will make your friendships so strong it'll be as if you and your friends are inseparable. Here are five of these magnetic qualities.

1. Authenticity

The first quality that attracts friends is authenticity. Authenticity is a big word that just means being "real." People like things that are the real deal. A diamond ring is much more valuable than cubic zirconia, and a Taylor guitar is much more valuable than some plastic knockoff from Wal-Mart™. Right? Why are they so much more valuable and desirable? It's because they are the real deal.

It's the same with friendship and fitting in. You are going to have a much better chance of having people want to hang with you if you are authentic. If you are into punk rock, then be into punk rock. If you love football, then love football. If you are a Christian with high moral standards, then live those standards every single day no matter where you are or whom you are with.

Just like diamonds, Taylor guitars, or designer jeans, the more real you are, the more valuable you will become to the people around you.

2. Giving

The second quality that attracts friends is giving. Jesus once said, "Give and it will be given to you" (Luke 6:38). When we hear these words, we generally think Jesus was talking about money, but, truth be told, the context in which Jesus made that statement was not about money at all. It was actually about friendship and the way we treat the people around us.

You see, whatever you give the people around you, they will give right back to you. If you give them a "Hello," they will say, "Hello," right back. If you give them a smile, you will get a smile from them. If you give them a compliment, they will thank you and compliment you as well.

Everyone loves a giver. So if you want to attract some friends, give your friendship away, and people will give it right back to you.

3. Happiness

Happiness is the third quality that attracts friends. Happiness is contagious, isn't it? Have you ever been to someone's house and something happens, and all of a sudden one person starts busting out laughing? And when I say laughing, I'm not talking about a little chuckle; I'm talking about a rolling-on-the-floor, snorting-like-a-pig, belly laugh.

When that happens, what do the people around them do? Do they roll their eyes and say, "What a moron! What in the world is wrong with that idiot?"

No. What do they do? They start to laugh. Then another person laughs. Then another and another, and before you know it, the entire room is rolling on the floor busting a gut. Why? Because happiness is contagious.

People like to be around people who are happy. So if you want people to be around you, lighten up, smile, and maybe even laugh a little. Who knows? You just might gain a friend.

4. Honesty

The fourth quality that attracts friends is honesty. The key to having a strong house that's able to withstand some serious storms is a good foundation. The foundation of friendship is honesty. Honesty is a very rare commodity these days; however, it is honesty that will help your friendships withstand the toughest storms.

You see, people know that you are going to make a bonehead mistake from time to time. People know you'll mess up. People know you will let them down someday and not always be perfect. However, if in spite of any or all of your shortcomings, people trust you and know you will always tell them the truth, they will always want to be your friend.

5. Faithfulness

Faithfulness is the fifth quality that attracts friends. Proverbs 17:17 says, "A friend loves at all times, and a brother is born for adversity."

Have you ever known bandwagon sports fans? You know the type, the ones who didn't have any allegiance to a team until that team started winning. But once the winning streak started and the team got on a roll, all of a sudden, out of nowhere, they start rocking the team's baseball cap and T-shirt, and they're watching every game on TV.

Is that person a real fan? No, absolutely not. You see, a real fan is the guy who has season tickets. A real fan has watched every game for the past ten years. A real fan has cheered through five losing seasons and still knows every player's name on the team. A real fan is the guy who wears the team T-shirt in spite of being made fun of. A real fan is faithful to his team no matter what.

The same is true for a real friend. A true friend is not a bandwagon friend who only comes around when there is a party going on or things are great. No, a true friend is someone who is faithful even when there is no party, when things aren't the best, when everyone else has left and the friendship is a little tense. That is a true friend. That is the type of person people want to have close to them.

Here's the thing about fitting in: you are not always going to. There are going to be some people who you just don't click with, and you know what, that is okay. That is normal.

If you will stop trying to do anything and everything to fit in, and simply begin to cultivate qualities that attract people—authenticity, happiness, generosity, honesty, and faithfulness—you will be the very definition of a friend. And because of that, you will begin to attract the right people at the right time.

What Do I
Do When...

My Friends
Are a Bad
Influence?

The world we live in is full of positive and negative charges. You learned about all that in science class, so I don't need to bore you with all those messy details. Right? Good. Well, when it comes to positive and negative charges, what about your friends? What kind of charges are they supplying you with?

Do yourself a favor. Stop reading for just a minute, and go grab a piece of paper and a pen. Go ahead. Stop reading and get what you need, then come back.

Do you have it? Great.

Now what I want you to do is write down your top ten closest friends. The friends you write down need to be the people in your inner circle, your closest friends. Go ahead. Take a minute or two, and write them down.

Do you have them?

Good.

As you start to move down your list, I want you to think about all the things your friends have said, the things they've done, and the ways they've acted toward you or the people around you this week.

As you're thinking of those things, write down a plus sign (+) or a minus sign (-) beside each name. Now be honest. Are the things they've done this week good or bad? Are they positive or negative?

One thing we never want to admit about ourselves, or anyone else for that matter, is that what we do defines who we are. If you steal, you are a thief. If you lie, you are a liar. If you give to the needy, you are by definition a giver. Who and what you are is defined by all the things you do.

Now with that thought in mind, look at your paper once again. Do any of your friends' names have a minus sign beside their names? If so, they are by definition a negative influence on you.

Three Responses to a Negative Influence

So what do you do when you have a friend, someone you enjoy being around, who is a negative influence on you? Well, here are three ideas.

1. Be Honest With Yourself

The first response you need to make when you realize your friends are a negative influence is to be honest with yourself. This sounds pretty simple, but it can be one of the hardest things to do because when it comes to people, we want to look at the qualities we like in them. We might say, "They're funny, they're very dependable, and they always listen to me when I need to talk to them." Those things are great, and likely true. However,

you have to be honest with yourself and realize where they're taking you.

If you were in a car that had a great paint job, some sweet tires, and a rockin' stereo system, would you want to ride in it? Sure, you would. Now, what if that car you were in, with all the cool stuff, was headed right for a four hundred-foot cliff on the side of a mountain? Would you still want to stay in the car? Let me just say, I hope not.

You see, it's the same way with your friend. They very well may have some amazing qualities. However, if they are taking you to parties you should not go to, Internet sites you should not visit, or further away from God instead of closer to Him, they are headed for a cliff, and if you're not honest with yourself, you are heading for some serious pain.

2. Control Your Environment

The second thing you need to do if your friends are a negative influence is to be in control of the environments you're in together. Here's what I mean by that. On the weekends, have them come over to your house instead of going over to theirs. When they ask you what movie you want to go see or what you want to do, don't say, "Oh, I don't care. Whatever you want." No, you pick the movie, you choose the agenda, and you control where you are going and what you are going to do. If they want

to do something or go to some places that aren't good, be strong enough to politely say, "No, I'm not going."

When your friends see that you are pretty set on what you're going to do and not do, usually they will give in and do it your way, which will keep you and them out of trouble.

3. Get Out of the Friendship Car

If you've been honest with yourself and tried to control the environments you're in with your friends who are a negative influence, the third thing you need to do is get out of the friendship car. This is the tough part. If you have friends who are a negative influence on you and you've tried to control the environments you put yourself in, but for whatever reason, things aren't changing, you need to open the door and get out of the friendship car.

I know. I know. You're best friends. You've known them for years. You've been through so much together. You can't just stop hanging out. That would be so mean, so rude.

Well, here's the deal. If you don't get out of the friendship, then within a few months, they will drive you off the four hundred-foot cliff that they are headed for. If that's what you want, then by all means stay where you are. However, if it's not, you need to start saying no.

"Do you want to go to the movies tonight?"

"No, sorry."

"Do you want to go to the party?"

"No, sorry."

"Do you want to come over and spend the night?"

"No."

"Do you want to..."

"No."

Unless their elevator doesn't go all the way to the top, eventually they will see that you don't want to hang out with them anymore, and they'll move on.

You don't have to be rude. You don't have to be mean. You don't have to get all up in their face. You can still be friendly. You can still love them like Jesus loves them. However, until they start making some serious changes, which would be nothing short of a one hundred eighty-degree turnaround, you need get out of the friendship car completely.

In review, what do you do when your friend is a negative influence on you? Be honest with yourself, start controlling your environments, and if that doesn't work, get out of the friendship car completely.

What Do I
Do When...

My Friend's
Getting
Into Some
Bad Stuff?

Maybe you're not into hiking, but for the sake of this example, let's just say that you are. So let's say you and your friend decide to go hiking at this huge state park a few hours away from your house. You've got all the gear you'll ever need— backpack, water, food, good boots, some rope—and you're totally good to go.

So you get to the state park and start to hike. Things are going great. You're laughing, talking, having a great time. About one hour into the hike, you guys are up in no man's land. The hills are beautiful. You're walking up a small trail on the very ledge of a cliff. No one's around for miles, and you're having the time of your life.

Then all of a sudden your friend's footing slips, and he slides down the cliff. His feet barely catch on a teeny tiny rock ledge about thirty feet below the trail you're standing on.

What do you do?

Do you say, "Dude, that is a bad break—see ya later," and walk away? Do you throw him some of your rope and a bottle of water and then walk away? Or do you figure out what would be the best way to help your friend and then begin to implement your plan?

Well, let me just say that I hope you choose option number three, because if you don't, you are not only a bad friend, but you are probably a little warped in the cranium.

You see, in reality you and your friend are on a journey called life, and most of the time the trail you're walking on isn't going to be green grass, plush meadows, and easy walking. No, the trail of the teenage years is pretty tumultuous terrain.

Maybe you have come to a point on your hike between the ages of thirteen to nineteen where some of your friends have slipped and fallen down a pretty steep cliff. Maybe they used to be the real deal; they knew who they were and were never afraid to live that way, but now they're living totally different lives.

Maybe some of your friends have been rockin' the church thing pretty solid as long as you've known them, but now— and you're not sure why—they are starting to miss church and really getting unplugged from it altogether.

Maybe your friend finally got a date, you knew things were getting pretty serious, but now you're noticing some big-time changes. The two are always together. They're always alone, and you're pretty sure that when they go to each other's house to "study" for two hours, the school books aren't even getting opened.

In these situations, what do you do? What should you do? Well, it's the same thing as going on a real hike and your friend has fallen off the cliff. He's not where he should be, and he needs some help.

If you just walk away from your friends, or tell them you're praying for them and then leave them to figure out what to do on their own, you're a pretty sorry friend. Right?

Well, I'm sure that's not you. If you have friends who are getting into some bad stuff, I'm sure you probably want to do something to help them out of the mess they're in, but maybe you're just not sure what to do. Well, over the next few pages, we're going to see if we can figure out a game plan for what to do when your friend is getting into some pretty bad stuff.

Skipping Out on Church

First, let's think about what you can do when your friends are skipping out on church. Now, skipping out or missing a church service every once in a while doesn't sound like that big of a deal. However, I heard a statement one time that I totally agree with: "The church is the hope of the world." You see, the church is the only organization on the planet that gives you the opportunity to connect with God, connect with friends, and make an eternal impact on your community. Hebrews 10:25 tells us, "Let us not give up meeting together...." Church is the real deal, and when people start to unplug from church, they will eventually begin to unplug from God.

That being said, it's easy for people to get out of the habit of going to church. Maybe they moved to a different part of town and now they have a longer drive. It could be that their parents decided to stop going, or maybe they're having some family problems and the entire family is skipping out on church. It also could be that your friend is just getting bored with being the good kid and going to church all the time. They might feel like they've done the church thing and now they want to see what the "real world" has to offer.

I don't know why your best buds haven't been coming to church. Chances are you don't either, so why not ask them?

1. Ask Them Why

If your friends have been skipping out on church, the first thing you need to do is ask why. So why haven't they been coming? Do you know? Have you asked? Why not? How hard would it be to just go up and say, "Hey, what's up? Noticed you've been bowing out of church for a few weeks. What's the deal?" If you'll ask, they just might tell you. Maybe they just haven't had a ride. If that's the case, you can give them one. Maybe they're getting a little bored with the whole church thing and just need a reason to come back. If so, what do you do?

2. Give Them a Reason To Come

After you've found out why your friends haven't been coming to church lately, give them a reason to come. You're their friend, so make church one of the places you hang out. Have some fun, learn a little bit about God, and then go grab some grub together afterward. Maybe talk to them about getting involved somewhere at church. At Oneighty®, we have students who help with our café, worship team, drama and video team, small groups, sound crew, and the list goes on and on. I'm sure your youth ministry has some places for you and your friend to get involved. Serving is a great way for you and your friend to make an impact, while at the same time gaining some friends and having a lot of fun.

Your friend needs you. Church isn't supposed to be all about you. Use it as an opportunity to keep your friend plugged into something that is going to help give them direction, purpose and what this world needs most…a little hope.

Living Two Lifestyles

Second, let's think about what to do if your friend is living two lifestyles. Around the age of fourteen, Christians start to realize that if they are going to be a Christian they are going to have to live a lot differently than the people around them. Doing the church and Christian thing was pretty easy in elementary school because all the kids were just like you, and the toughest thing about life was who was going to get to the swings first at recess.

But life is a little different now. Things aren't so easy, and the desire to always fit in often drives well-intentioned people to live two lifestyles. At church, they are all Jesus junky—nice shirt, nice smile, and nice attitude. But at school, they turn into a totally different person.

This is a very common thing in Christian culture. It's not right, but it's very common. So what do you do when your friend is living two lifestyles?

1. Make Sure You Are Not

If your friend is living two lifestyles, the first thing you have to do is make sure you are not. I'm going to ask you a question: What's up with you? How is your walk with Christ going? I'm not talking about your walk with Christ that everyone sees; I'm talking about you—the real you. The one you see in the mirror every day. What's up with you? Are you the real deal? If you have a friend who's living two lives, this is a good time for you to do some self evaluation. Look in the mirror, and make sure you are the real deal.

2. Have the Tough Conversation

Once you've taken a good long look in the mirror and know everything is good with you, then it's time to have the tough conversation with your friend who's living two lifestyles. This is never easy, but you have to do it. Too many times we see a friend who is doing the double life thing and we just hope they change. We refuse to talk to them about it because we think, *Who am I to tell them how to live?* Or we think, *I can't say anything. They'll get mad at me.*

You know what? Those are just excuses that keep you from helping a friend who is in some serious trouble. If you were doing something that was going to jack your life up, would you want someone to at least care enough about you to confront you with your problem? Sure, you would. So man up (or woman up), stop making excuses, be a true friend, and have the tough conversation.

3. Help Them Change

Okay, you're doing great in your walk with Christ. You've confronted your friends about the issues of living two lifestyles. Now it's time to take the third step of helping them change.

How? Do whatever it takes. If your friend is getting into the party scene, start partying with them. No, don't have a big kegger at your house, but make you and your good group of friends the people they hang out with. Instead of them going somewhere else for a good time, you become the good time—minus the booze.

Now, if your friends are getting into some heavy stuff, like big-time drinking or drugs, you have to get some adults involved. Encourage them to have a good long talk with their parents or get some counseling. This is too big for you to handle, so help them get some professional help.

Regardless of what issues they're struggling with, you are their friend. So do whatever it takes to help them change.

Becoming Sexually Active

Third, let's think about what to do if your friend is becoming sexually active. Have you ever sat down in your living room, turned on the TV, and grabbed a soda and a bag of potato chips? Sure, you have. Man, that is great stuff. Feeding your face while watching a good movie is tons of fun. Right? Okay, let me ask you this: In that situation, have you ever opened up a bag of chips, eaten one chip, closed the bag, and put it back on the shelf, saving it for later? No? Me neither. That's pretty tough to do, isn't it?

Well, I've got to be honest with you and say that is the exact situation your sexually active friends have put themselves in. They are enjoying all the kissy kissy, touchy touchy they can, and just like us with that bag of potato chips, they can't wait to go back and get some more.

Now, I'm not saying it's impossible for these friends to put sex completely on the shelf altogether until they get married, because they can. It's been done before and will happen again. However, the truth of the matter is that it's not going to be easy.

First of all, your friends have to want to stop. You can talk to them all you want, but unless they know it's wrong and want

to stop, they won't stop. When it comes to your friends'
private sex lives, there are only so many things you can do,
and here are some of them.

How to Help Them S.T.O.P.

1. Sit Down and Talk

When you realize your friends are becoming sexually
active, the first thing you should do is sit down and talk.
This could be a very awkward thing to do, but if you're
worried about your best friends, you owe it to them to sit
down and talk about what's going on. Ask them point-
blank what the deal is, how far they've gone, and why. Let
them know God's standard of purity, that they are messing
up, but you love them anyway and you want to help
however you can. You know what? They may take you up
on it and start on the journey to sexual purity. However,
they may look at you and say, "It's none of your business,"
and keep doing what they want. Either way, you have let
them know where you stand and they can trust you.

2. Take Your Stand

The second thing you need to do is to take your stand on
sexual purity. What do you think is right? What do you
think is wrong? What do you and your special somebody
do when you're all alone? If you have friends who are
messing up and you want to help them, you need to

make sure you're living the way you need to live. Sit down this week and write out what your standards are for sexual purity. Then live by them.

3. Offer Some Advice

Third, if your friends are becoming sexually active, you should prepare yourself to offer some advice. Knowledge is power. Your friends need to know what the truth is, not just what their bodies are telling them. Here are a few books that are packed with advice on all things sexual purity.

- *What Do I Do When? Answering Your Toughest Questions About Sex* (This isn't a bad book. In fact, I know the author.)

- *Uncensored—Dating, Friendship, and Sex: You Think You Know, But You Have No Idea* by Jeanie Mayo

- *Dateable: Are You? Are They?* by Justin Lookadoo and Hayley DiMarco

These books are full of great stories, Scriptures, and insight on how to have a great dating life without getting involved in sex. Pick up a few of these books and read them for yourself. After you've read them, talk to your friends about what you learned or, better yet, give the books to them so they can give them a read. Either way, they will be getting some good advice.

4. Pray

Prayer is something we should always do; however, in this
situation when you're concerned about friends being sexually active, prayer is probably the most important thing
you can do. Your friends are in way over their heads, and
they need more help than you can give them. If they're
ever going to have the strength to completely shelf sex
until they're married, they'll have to experience a true
change of heart. God is the only person who can trans-
form someone from the inside out, so begin to make it a
daily habit to go to God in prayer for your friends.

What Do I
Do When...

I'm Jealous
of My Friend?

When I was in high school, I knew a guy we'll call Alex. Alex's family was flat-out loaded. His father owned a very successful business and was extremely wealthy. Because of this, Alex always had the latest and greatest of everything.

When I say everything, I mean everything. Huge house, designer jeans, shirts, shoes, watches, video game systems— you name it, Alex had it.

To put this story into perspective, I'll add that during Alex's sophomore year, his father purchased a brand-new Camaro Z28 to give him as a gift for when he got his driver's license. During his junior year, Alex drove a brand new Lamborghini. And for a graduation present, he was given a brand new Ferrari Testarossa. Yeah, you read that right—a brand new Ferrari. The dude was only eighteen years old and had a Camaro, a Lamborghini, and a Ferrari. Like I said, Alex's father worked very hard and was very wealthy.

I have to be honest and admit that although we were some-what friendly with each other, I didn't like Alex very much. In my mind and to my other friends, I would say things like, "Alex is a lot different than I am. We have different friends. We don't have a lot of classes together, and that's why I just don't care for him that much."

However, the ugly fact of the matter was that I was jealous of Alex. I was jealous of the fact that his family was so wealthy. I was jealous of the fact that every day he could drive any one of his three mucho expensive cars to school. All the while the only option I had was my bright red 1983 Chevy Citation Hatchback that was anything but a chick magnet, if you know what I mean.

Oh, my family was very well taken care of, and I never lacked for anything at all when I was growing up. In fact, my car actually wasn't that bad and my parents bought it for me as a gift when I got my driver's license. But at the time, none of that mattered. Alex had what I wanted. Alex had what I didn't have, and I was jealous.

What do you do when you're jealous of a friend?

Girls, what do you do when your friend is just drop-dead gorgeous? She puts on anything and looks amazing no matter what she's wearing. She walks on the beach in a two-piece bikini and everyone stops and stares because she's so beautiful. But every time you put on your bathing suit, you can barely even look at yourself in the mirror.

What do you do when you're jealous of a friend?

Guys, what do you do when your buddy is just a flat-out athletic stud? He's strong, fast, and jumps through the roof. Coaches love him, and girls think he's a Greek god.

What do you do when you're jealous of a friend?

What do you do when your friend lives in a house that's way nicer than yours, or rides or drives in cars that blow the doors off of your ride? What do you do when your friends have what you want? What do you do when you're jealous of a friend?

Realize How Sick Jealousy Actually Is

If you're jealous of a friend, the first thing you need to do is realize how sick jealousy is. Proverbs 14:30 says, "A heart at peace gives life to the body, but envy rots the bones." When you have friends you're jealous of because they are better looking than you, have more money than you, have a better family life than you, or have way better grades than yours, Scripture says this emotion, this feeling, like a disease, will begin to rot you from the inside out.

Jealousy is more than an emotion you shouldn't have. It is a gross and destructive force. Here's the thing about jealousy that's so rotten, when you have someone you're jealous or envious of, the only thing the other person can do to make you feel better is fail in some way.

If they just got a new phone, the only way they can make you feel better is by losing the phone or breaking it somehow. If you have a friend who is beautiful and skinny, the only way she can make you feel better is to start shoving Twinkies in her face and gain thirty pounds. If you know someone who has very wealthy parents, much like my friend Alex, the only thing he can do to make you feel better about yourself is to lose everything he has.

Now stop and think about that for a minute. That is really sick and demented. That's jealousy!

Jealousy is a gross monster living deep inside of us that wants negative things to happen to other people. Jealousy is something that we should want absolutely no part of.

The Problem Isn't Your Friend

If you're jealous of a friend, the second thing you need to do is realize the problem isn't your friend.

Years ago, my brother and I went through a phase where we got scared almost every single night. The reason was that we had been watching these movies at our church about the end of time and the tribulation period with the antichrist, the mark of the beast, and all of that scary stuff. So every time we heard even a little tiny creak in the floor, we were both sure the beast was coming to get us.

Most nights, either I would end up in Brian's bed or he would end up in mine. I remember thinking one night, *I'm going to get in bed with him tonight and save myself a trip.*

We both said our prayers and lay down in bed. I'm not sure what Brian was thinking about, but I was thinking about Jesus coming back, the rapture, and this crazy man called the beast. I was getting pretty scared already.

Well, we both finally dozed off into a deep sleep, when all of a sudden, my brother sat up in the bed and screamed, "AAAAAAAAAHHHHHH! AAAAAAAAAHHHHHHH! AAAAAAAAAHHHHHHH!"

I jumped up out of the bed and screamed in an extremely deep voice that scared me when it came out, "BRIAN, WHAT'S WRONG? BRIAN...BRIAN, WHAT'S WRONG?"

Now we were both scared to death—Brian because he saw someone staring at him through the window and me because I sounded like a demon-possessed boy. Needless to say, it was a crazy night.

My mom and dad came running into the room and quickly discovered that there was no one outside the window at all. What had happened was Brian had woken up, sat up in bed, and had seen his own reflection in the window.

That night, the issue wasn't someone else; the issue was Brian's reflection.

It's the same way with your jealousy issue. When you look at someone else and see the car they drive, the money they spend, or the attention they get, you think the problem is with them. But in actuality, the problem is with you.

You see, if you were totally honest, you would have to admit that there is nothing wrong with them having any or all of those things they have. The problem is that you don't have the things they have and you want them.

You don't have that car. You don't have that body. You don't get that much attention. You don't have what they have, and that is the real problem.

So when you are jealous of someone, when you look at them, you are not seeing them at all. You are actually seeing yourself. You are seeing what you want. You are seeing what you need. You are seeing what you think you can never have. The more you look at them, the more you are actually looking at yourself, and that nasty creature lurking deep inside your heart keeps getting bigger and bigger.

Kill the Jealousy Monster

If you're jealous of a friend, the third thing you need to do is kill the jealousy monster.

I have to be honest and admit that I used to have a real jealousy problem. Not just with Alex, but with all of my friends. When someone had something, anything that I didn't have, I would not say anything to them about it, but deep inside of me, it was there. I was jealous.

Here are a couple things I started doing to kill the jealousy monster inside of me. If you have a friend you are a little bit jealous of, these "jealousy monster killers" will help you out as well.

Celebrate Other People's Good Fortune

So you want to slay the jealousy monster? The first step is to celebrate someone's good fortune. I've made a habit of this one. As soon as I see someone with something really nice or maybe even new, I instantly walk up to them and ask them about it and congratulate them on their good fortune.

One time a few years ago, I was driving a small two-door hatchback. Now, you may not know it, but I am not a small guy. I'm about six foot one, and two hundred forty pounds. Every day I was crunching into this tiny little car to go back and forth to my office at the church. It was a nice little car. God really provided a miracle when we got it (that's another story for another book); however, it was just kind of small and about ten years old.

Well, one day I was driving up to the church office and I noticed that one of my buddies at church was pulling up in a sweet, brand-new, black, four-door pickup truck. Man, this thing was decked out. It was a really sweet ride. It was exactly what I had wanted.

Well, I parked my car, walked right up to him, shook his hand, and said, "Dude, did you just get this? Man, it's unbelievable! Congratulations. I'm really happy for you." I got in the truck, looked around, bragged about it a little more, shook his hand one more time, and then walked away.

Then I opened up the door of my little red car and drove off. As I pulled out of the parking lot, I remember thanking God for blessing my friend with such a nice vehicle.

You may be reading this and thinking, *Kevin, how could you do that? He had an amazing truck, and you had a little red vehicle. He was driving around in a sprawling four-wheel drive, and you were crunched up in a compact car.*

Well, the Bible says in Philippians 4:19, "My God will meet all your needs according to his glorious riches in Christ Jesus." So the reason I'm able to be happy when someone else receives God's provision is that I know the God who gave my friend a great truck is the same God who will supply all of my needs as well.

Today I still own that little red car God blessed us with. I gave it to my son, and today I drive a black, four-door SUV that God supplied for me.

Let me ask you a question. How do you respond when one of your friends has some new shoes, new clothes, a new car, or something you would love to have? If you do anything other than go up to them and tell them, "Congrats," you are flat-out

missing it, because the same God who loves them loves you.
The same God who provided for them will provide for you. The
same God who gave them the opportunity to get something
they needed wants to do the same thing for you.

So the next time something good happens to your friends,
don't be jealous. Be happy for them, knowing that God wants
to bless you, too.

Live a Life That God Can Bless

The second way to slay the jealousy monster is to live a life
that God can bless. When it comes to your friends and things
they have, there is absolutely no reason for you to be jealous.
If you will begin to obey God and live your life the way He
says to live it, He will begin to bless your money, your body,
your family, and everything else that you have. This is the
second way to kill the monster of jealousy—living a life that
God can bless.

Look at this Scripture:

> If you fully obey the LORD your God and carefully
> follow all his commands I give you today, the LORD
> your God will set you high above all the nations on
> earth. All these blessings will come upon you and
> accompany you if you obey the LORD your God: You
> will be blessed in the city and blessed in the country.
> The fruit of your womb will be blessed, and the crops

of your land and the young of your livestock—the calves of your herds and the lambs of your flocks. Your basket and your kneading trough will be blessed. You will be blessed when you come in and blessed when you go out. The LORD will grant that the enemies who rise up against you will be defeated before you. They will come at you from one direction but flee from you in seven. The LORD will send a blessing on your barns and on everything you put your hand to. The LORD your God will bless you in the land he is giving you.

Deuteronomy 28:1-8

God will bless you when you obey. Here are four areas where you'll see His blessing.

1. Money

When you obey God, He will bless you with the things you need, including money. Proverbs 21:5 says, "The plans of the diligent lead to profit."

Remember my friend Alex, whom I mentioned earlier—the one with three sweet rides? He is living proof that when you obey God's Word, you will be blessed. Alex's father worked extremely hard and was a very good business-man. He knew what he wanted and was not afraid to work hard to get it. His plans to succeed and willingness to work led him to profit—and a lot of it.

It is the same with you. What do you want? Do you want a nice car, a new shirt, an Xbox 360, or an iPhone? That's great. There's nothing wrong with wanting those things, but how are you going to get them? Scripture says that if you make plans and work hard, you will profit. You will get the things you want.

So stop hating on your buddy who has all the stuff you want. Get up, start working, and you can have them, too.

2. Body

When you obey God, He will bless you in how your body looks and works. Okay, let's face it, some people are genetic freaks. They were born with six-pack abs, thin hips, and a beautiful smile. It's easy to hate those people because they're beautiful. Right?

But you know what? Most people aren't that way. The people I know who look good, work hard to look good. They watch what they eat, exercise at least a little bit, and take care of themselves. I've found it's pretty easy to sit around complaining that we don't look as good as so-and-so while we're drinking Mountain Dew® and stuffing our faces with Cheetos®.

You control your own destiny. If you want to be a little thinner or get in a little better shape, start working out, exercise a little bit, and watch what you eat. You'll be amazed how quickly you morph into the person you want to be.

3. Stuff

If you obey God, He will bless you with stuff. So let me take a wild guess. Your friends have some stuff you want, but don't have. Because of this, you are a little bit jealous of them. Now, you've never told them, but the jealousy is there. Every time you see them with all the stuff you want to have, deep inside, you're upset; you're a little jealous.

We all want stuff, don't we? New shoes, new clothes, new video game systems, new cars, new hats, new phones, new shirts, new guitars—the list goes on and on. We all want more!

Well, here's a little something you need to know about getting more. The secret to getting more is taking care of what you already have. Listen to what Jesus said in Luke 16:10: "Whoever can be trusted with very little can also be trusted with much, and whoever is dishonest with very little will also be dishonest with much."

Did you catch what Jesus was throwing at you in this verse? If you have been faithful with the little things, you will be faithful with more.

If you want the new phone that just came out, but you're constantly misplacing or breaking the one you already have, your parents won't be too hyped on running out and buying you something else that you can trash or ruin. They want to see you take care of what you already have before they'll get you something else.

So stop hating on someone who has been given more than what you have. If you will start taking care of your stuff, you just might get a little more.

4. Attention

If you obey God, He will bless you with attention from others. Proverbs 22:29 says, "Do you see a man skilled in his work? He will serve before kings; he will not serve before obscure men."

This is one of my favorite passages in the entire Bible. What it's basically saying is that if someone becomes very good at what they do—maybe it's sports, algebra, singing, dancing, acting, writing, or anything at all—eventually people like coaches, teachers, employers, and friends will start to pay attention to him.

If you have a friend who's getting a lot of attention, is it because they are a jerk? Or it is because they're pretty good at something? Maybe they're a good listener, so people like to talk to them. Maybe they're really funny, so people like to listen to them. Maybe they can flat-out drill someone on the football field, so the coaches see potential in them.

When someone else gets the attention we want, it's very easy to start picking them apart and say how unfair it is. But in reality, all that's happening is that Proverbs 22:29 is coming to pass. Their skills are bringing them attention.

So what are you good at? What skills do you have? It can be anything—anything at all. If you will start honing in and becoming great at those things, eventually people will begin to notice you.

An End to the Jealousy Monster

It can be so easy to become jealous of a friend. But in reality, there's no reason to let the ugly disease begin to fester and grow deep inside of you. If you've found yourself feeling a little jealous of some people you're close to, understand they are not the problem at all. Know that God wants to bless you just as He did them. Congratulate them on their success, and begin to live a life that God can bless. If you'll do these things, you will shove a stake through the heart of the ugly monster of jealousy once and for all.

Conclusion

Friendship can be really wonderful, and it can be really hard. Sometimes your friends don't want Jesus. Sometimes they're mean. Sometimes they stab you in the back. Sometimes it's hard to fit in. Sometimes they're a bad influence and get into bad stuff, and sometimes it's hard not to be jealous of them.

Despite the fact that friendship can be so challenging, it's something we all want and need. It's my prayer that through this book, you've learned some good methods for creating strong friendships that help you grow as a person and also lead others to the best friend of all—Jesus.

Prayer of Salvation

God loves you—no matter who you are, no matter what your past. God loves you so much that He gave His one and only begotten Son for you. The Bible tells us that "...whoever believes in him shall not perish but have eternal life" (John 3:16). Jesus laid down His life and rose again so that we could spend eternity with Him in heaven and experience His absolute best on earth. If you would like to receive Jesus into your life, say the following prayer out loud and mean it from your heart.

Heavenly Father, I come to You admitting that I am a sinner. Right now, I choose to turn away from sin, and I ask You to cleanse me of all unrighteousness. I believe that Your Son, Jesus, died on the cross to take away my sins. I also believe that He rose again from the dead so that I might be forgiven of my sins and made righteous through faith in Him. I call upon the name of Jesus Christ to be the Savior and Lord of my life. Jesus, I choose to follow You and ask that You fill me with the power of the Holy Spirit. I declare that right now I am a child of God. I am free from sin and full of the righteousness of God. I am saved in Jesus' name. Amen.

If you prayed this prayer to receive Jesus Christ as your Savior for the first time, please contact us on the web at **www.harrisonhouse.com** to receive a free book.

Or you may write to us at

Harrison House

P.O. Box 35035

Tulsa, Oklahoma 74153

About Kevin Moore

Kevin Moore is the youth pastor of Oneighty®, the youth ministry of Church on the Move in Tulsa, Oklahoma. With more than 16 years experience in youth ministry, Kevin's passion in life is to introduce teenagers to the person of Jesus Christ and help them walk out their faith in a real and personal way.

Throughout the year, Kevin travels and speaks at leadership and student conferences around nation. The biblical principles he shares are proven to work in any size church or city.

Kevin and his wife Veronica have been married for 17 years. They have four children: Jordan 16, Logan 13, Mikayla 9, and Lilly Grace, 1 year old.

You can contact Kevin Moore at
growmoore@gmail.com
www.twitter.com/kevinmoore180
www.facebook.com/kevinmoore180
Kevin Moore P.O. Box 692032
Tulsa, OK 74169-2032

Read Kevin's blog at www.kevinmoore.tumblr.com

*Please include your prayer requests
and comments when you write.*

Other Books in the What Do I Do When? Series

What Do I Do When—Answering Your Toughest Questions About God

Kevin Moore encourages you to seek God for yourself in the Scriptures and in your own heart, plus answers questions like: "Why do bad things happen to good people?" and "What do I do when I'm a Christian but the feelings are gone?" You will discover amazing things about God

and learn a lot about yourself along the way.

What Do I Do When?

Answering Your Toughest Questions About God

978-1-57794-959-6

What Do I Do When...Money

Moore counsels you that you cannot identify yourself by what you have, that loving money is a big mistake, and what you can do to guard your heart against greed. You will gain a great foundation to build your future on, putting

God first and using money as a tool to achieve your dreams.

What Do I Do When?

Answering Your Toughest Questions About Money

978-1-57794-960-2

What Do I Do When—Answering Your
Toughest Questions About
Sex, Love, and Dating

From questions like "What do I do when my parents won't
let me date?" to "What do I do when my date wants to get
physical?" you will find the answers backed by God's Word

and in the context that addresses
today's issues.

What Do I Do When?

Answering Your Toughest Questions
About Sex, Love, and Dating

978-1-57794-961-9

Available at bookstores everywhere
or visit **www.harrisonhouse.com**

The Harrison House Vision

Proclaiming the truth and the power

Of the Gospel of Jesus Christ

With excellence;

Challenging Christians to

Live victoriously,

Grow spiritually,

Know God intimately.